Baby Cross Stitch

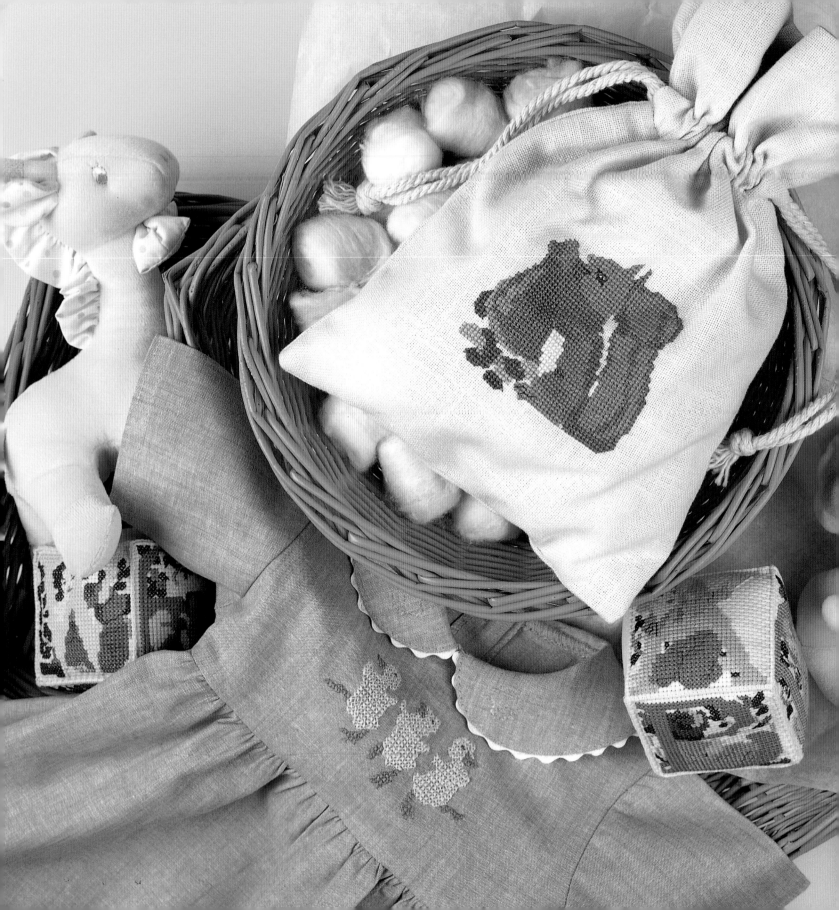

Baby Cross Stitch

OVER 40 CAPTIVATING DESIGNS

CHRIS TIMMS

HAMLYN

This book is dedicated to my five grandchildren
Rhiannnon and Joshua Atkins, Daisy and Flora Hamilton and Bethany Pearson

BABY CROSS STITCH
Chris Timms

This edition published in 1996
by Hamlyn
an imprint of Reed International Books Limited
Michelin House, 81 Fulham Road, London, SW3 6RB
and Auckland, Melbourne, Singapore and Toronto

© Text and embroidery designs Chris Timms 1996
© Photographs Reed International Books Limited 1996

Art Editor LISA TAI
Editor SAMANTHA GRAY
Executive Editor SIMON TUITE
Design Manager BRYAN DUNN
Art Editor MARK STEVENS
Photography DEBI TRELOAR
Styling FRANCESCA MILLS
Illustrations JANE HUGHES
Production CANDIDA LANE

A CIP record for this book is available from the British Library

ISBN 0 600 58806 8
ISBN 0 600 58996 X *(paperback)*

The publishers have made very effort to ensure that all instructions given in this book are accurate and safe, but they cannot accept liability for any resulting injury, damage or loss to either person or property whether direct or consequential and howsoever arising. The author and publishers will be grateful for any information which will assist them in keeping future editions up to date.

Typeset in Caslon 540 Roman, Caslon 3, Kuenstler Script Medium

Colour origination by Mandarin Offset, Singapore
Produced by Mandarin Offset
Printed and bound in Hong Kong

Contents

Foreword

I found expecting a child to be one of the most exciting events of my life and I know the pleasure involved in preparing for the new arrival to the family. For the first baby the excitement is perhaps the most acute. Part of the joy is in preparing clothes, bedclothes, crib and nursery. I found it extremely enjoyable choosing and buying the crib and bedding for my first baby. Every Saturday, throughout my first pregnancy, it was my treat to buy something for the baby – at frequent intervals afterwards, I used to get out the item from a specially painted chest of drawers to admire it. It was also exciting during my following pregnancies to get the crib down from the attic and reassemble it for its next occupant.

Many people like to make their own baby clothes. I made a lot for my first baby, but with subsequent babies there often isn't the time, so I have devoted a chapter to designs that you can cross stitch on to clothing bought from chain stores. This will quickly and simply transform a variety of garments and, although you may have bought similar clothes to other people, they will become special items.

Cross stitching is the ideal pursuit when you are in the later stages of pregnancy, as you can sit with your feet up and keep yourself profitably and creatively occupied while resting.

The book is divided into five chapters and covers the whole range of items you will want to cross stitch for your baby or grandchild.

The first chapter is devoted to cards and gift tags, the second to pictures and a sampler to brighten up the nursery. The third chapter provides a range of inspirational projects for clothes and the fourth includes a myriad of useful items to make for the nursery such as cushions, sheets, cot covers and bumpers, tie backs for the curtains, bags for the laundry and to carry toys, and nappy changing equipment. Finally, there are even some toys to make.

I hope you all enjoy your babies as much as I have done and happy stitching!

Cards and Gift Tags

Hand stitched cards are a lovely gift for a baby. Birth cards are usually kept for sentimental reasons anyway, but how much nicer to have one that has been lovingly hand stitched and can also be framed and hung on the wall as a memento.

All the designs on the following pages are mounted on to bought cards, but you can make your own to personalize the whole item. The card will itself form a mount if it is later framed. The designs are worked in pastel colours to fit in with the mood of the book but they would look equally good in bright or dark colours. You could also decorate bought cards if you want a different look. For instance, the cards I have used have a groove bordering the centre cut out – these could be filled in by ruling lines with a silver or gold pen. The card could also be lightly sponge painted in a pastel or metallic colour, or spattered by flicking paint from a paint brush. Alternatively, a stencil brush dipped into a small amount of paint and dabbed on to the card will give a pleasing, uneven smattering of colour. Experiment first on a spare piece of scrap paper or card until the desired effect is achieved. In addition, lace or ribbon can be stuck around the card to form a border, or cut a pretty frame cut for the design from a paper doily, or the doily used as a stencil.

This chapter contains designs for birth announcement cards for a boy and girl, first birthday cards for a boy and girl, a birth congratulations card, a Christmas card and two gift tag designs. The designs are worked on 14-,

16- and 18-count aida fabric and on 28-count evenweave fabric stitched over two threads each way (thus making 14-count) so there should be something to suit everybody. You can, of course, if you find it easier, work any of the designs on 14- or even 11-count fabric (but you will then need to use three strands of the stranded embroidery cotton to get a good coverage and the finished designs will be larger). The Chick Gift Tag is a good candidate for working on an 11-count fabric and could then be given as a small card if you are short of time or a beginner at cross stitch. It could be put into a hand made card for an even more personal touch.

Try out the designs on different coloured background fabrics too, and experiment with matching and contrasting card colours. The Birth Congratulations Card is worked on the palest blue 16-count fabric. As I have used very pale, subtle colouring for this design, the whole is outlined in light grey for definition. The Girl's Birth Announcement card shows a little dark haired girl engrossed in playing with her doll. The design is placed in a card with a circular mount which enhances its shape. This design was inspired by a drawing from a magazine in a very old scrapbook, and is also worked on 16-count aida fabric. The Boy's Birth Announcement card showing a golden haired baby boy holding a soft toy bunny is worked on 14-count aida fabric and was inspired by a drawing in the same scrapbook. The lad in pyjamas holding his teddy and rabbit is also worked on 14-count aida fabric and the girl triumphantly holding her new kitten up aloft on the Girl's First Birthday Card is worked on pink 28-count evenweave fabric. The girl under the Christmas tree excitedly opening her presents is worked on 18-count white aida fabric. This is the most complicated and time consuming of the cards. Worked on 14-count fabric, it would be larger and therefore make a delightful picture for the nursery wall.

Boy's Birth Announcement

A member of the family or a close friend would be delighted to receive this special, cross stitched card to announce the birth of a baby boy.

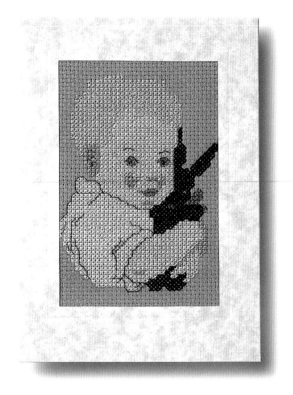

To make up

Following the chart and beginning centrally (see p.104), work the design in cross stitch using two strands of embroidery thread. Each square represents one cross stitch. Where squares are shown divided diagonally, work three-quarter cross stitches (see p.105). Add the outlining and facial features on the boy and rabbit in back stitch.

Press the completed work on the reverse using a hot iron setting (see p.106), then mount the card following the instructions on p.106.

Measurements

The actual cross stitch design measures 10 x 7.5cm (4 x 3in)

Materials

• Piece of blue 14-count aida fabric measuring 18 x 18cm (7 x 7in)
• DMC or Anchor stranded embroidery cotton, one skein each of the colours shown in the chart
• Tapestry needle, size 24
• Card with rectangular opening measuring 11 x 7cm (2¾ x 4⅓in)

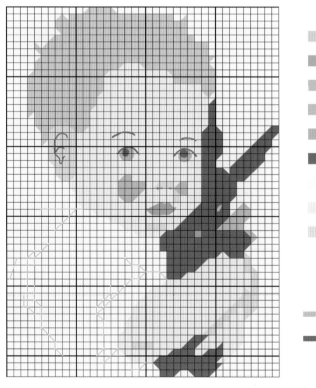

	DMC	Anchor
	677	398
	223	262
	224	260
	3816	398
	794	262
	3799	260
	ecru	398
	948	262
	950	260

Back stitch

	DMC	Anchor
	3042	870
	317	400

Girl's Birth Announcement

In this enchanting card, a little girl looks lovingly at the doll she is cradling in her arms.

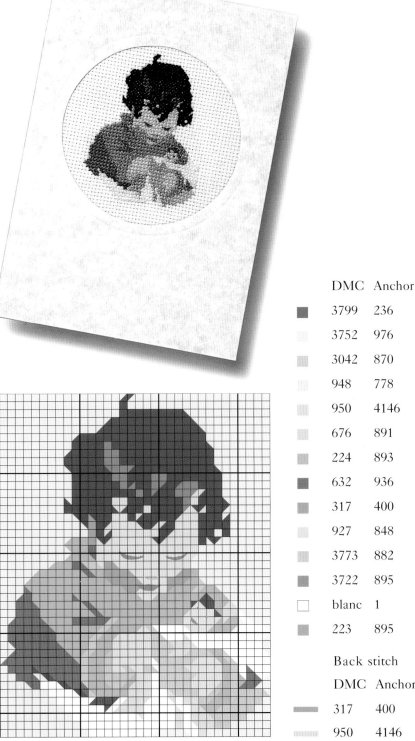

Measurements
The actual cross stitch design measures
6.5 x 5cm (2 x 2⅛in)

Materials
• Piece of cream 16-count aida fabric measuring
16 x 16cm (6¼ x 6¼in)
• DMC stranded embroidery cotton, one skein
each of the colours shown in the chart
• Tapestry needle, size 24

To make up
Following the chart and beginning centrally (see
p.104), work the design in cross stitch using two
strands of embroidery thread. Each square represents one cross stitch. Where squares are shown
divided diagonally, with half in one colour and
half in another, work three-quarter cross stitches
(see p.105). Embroider the facial features. The
little girl's eyes are worked in back stitch, using
deep blue embroidery thread, and the doll's eyes
are worked in French knots, using the same
colour as for the back stitching.

Press the completed work on the reverse side
using a hot iron setting (see p.106), then mount
the card following the instructions on p.106.

	DMC	Anchor
■	3799	236
	3752	976
	3042	870
	948	778
	950	4146
	676	891
	224	893
■	632	936
	317	400
	927	848
	3773	882
	3722	895
□	blanc	1
	223	895

Back stitch

	DMC	Anchor
—	317	400
⋯	950	4146

Boy's 1st Birthday Card

A baby boy holds a comforting, cuddly toy rabbit and teddy bear in this delightful birthday card.

Measurements
The actual cross stitch design measures
8.75 x 4cm (3.5 x 1.5in)

Materials
• Piece of grey-green 14-count aida fabric measuring 16.5 x 16.5cm (6½ x 6½in)
• DMC or Anchor stranded embroidery cotton, one skein each of the colours shown in the chart
• Tapestry needle, size 24
• Cream card with rectangular opening measuring 11 x 7cm (4⅓ x 2¾in)

To make up
Following the chart and beginning centrally (see p.104), work the design in cross stitch using two strands of embroidery thread. Each square represents one cross stitch. Where squares are shown divided diagonally, with half in one colour and half in another, work three-quarter and quarter cross stitches. Work the rabbit's eyes and nose in French knots using dark brown embroidery thread, and the boy's eye and ear outlining and the outlining of the bear's face in back stitch using brown and light brown threads.

Press the completed work on the reverse using a hot iron setting (see p.106), then mount the card following the instructions on p.106.

	DMC	Anchor
■	3807	177
■	791	178
■	729	890
■	3046	887
■	3722	895
■	3781	905
■	611	898
■	3042	870
■	948	778
☐	blanc	1
■	3768	779

Backstitch		
	DMC	Anchor
▬	791	178
▬	3781	398

Girl's 1st Birthday Card

A small girl with a smiling cat decorate this pretty birthday card, which is certain to be much appreciated.

Measurements
The actual design measures 6 x 9cm (2½ x 3½in)

Materials
• Piece of pink 28-count pink evenweave fabric measuring 16.5 x 16.5cm (6½ x 6½in)
• DMC or Anchor stranded embroidery cotton, one skein each of the colours in the chart
• Tapestry needle, size 26
• Pink card with oval opening measuring 10 x 8cm (4 x 3¼in)

To make up
Each square represents one cross stitch over two threads of fabric each way. Where squares are shown divided diagonally, with half in one colour and half in another, work three-quarter cross stitches (see p.105). When all the cross stitching is complete, add the facial features in back stitch and straight stitch using a single strand of embroidery thread. Work the iris of the eye in dark blue, the lips in pink, the eyebrows, nose, kitten's eyes, whiskers and facial outlining in grey.

Finally press the completed embroidery on the reverse side using a hot iron setting (see p.106), and then mount the card following the instructions that are given on p.106.

	DMC	Anchor
■	221	897
	932	343
	931	921
	948	778

	DMC	Anchor
	950	4146
■	420	374
	3045	888
■	3799	236
☐	blanc	1

Back stitch

	DMC	Anchor
—	3799	236
—	931	921
—	221	897

Birth Congratulations Card

Welcome the arrival of a new baby by cross stitching a card to celebrate the birth. This design is worked in pretty shades of pink, blue and yellow.

Measurements

The actual cross stitch design measures
8 x 4.25cm (3¼ x 1¾in)

Materials

• Piece of sky blue 16-count aida fabric, measuring 16 x 16cm (6½ x 6½in)
• DMC or Anchor stranded embroidery cotton, one skein each of the colours shown in the chart
• Tapestry needle, size 24
• Pale blue card with oval opening, measuring 8 x 10cm (3 x 4in)

To make up

Following the chart and beginning centrally (see p.104), work the design in cross stitch using two strands of thread. Each square represents one cross stitch. When the cross stitching is complete, add the outlining and features in back stitch.

Press the completed work on the reverse using a hot iron setting (see p.106), then mount the card following the instructions on p.104.

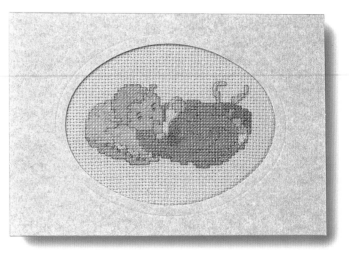

	DMC	Anchor		Back stitch	
				DMC	Anchor
	341	117			
	225	892		452	232
	948	778		3743	869
	677	300		340	118
	ecru	387		3042	870
	3743	869			
	blanc	1			

Christmas Card

A little girl sits besides a Christmas tree unwrapping her presents in this delightful, festive scene which is worked in shades of pink and green.

Measurements
The actual cross stitch design measures
7.5 x 6cm (2⅞ x 2⅓in)

Materials
• Piece of white 18-count aida fabric measuring
15 x 15cm (6 x 6in)
• DMC or Anchor stranded embroidery cotton,
one skein each of the colours shown in the chart

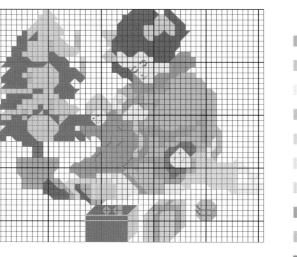

	DMC	Anchor
	407	914
	224	893
	948	778
	3041	871
	809	130
	950	4146
	834	874
	501	878
	502	877
	938	381
	839	360
	598	167
	597	168
	413	401

Back stitch

	DMC	Anchor
	413	401
	224	893
	502	877
	839	360

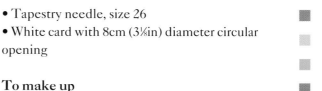

• Tapestry needle, size 26
• White card with 8cm (3⅛in) diameter circular opening

To make up
Following the chart and beginning centrally (see p. 104), work the design in cross stitch using two strands of embroidery thread. Each square represents one cross stitch. Where squares are shown divided diagonally, with half in one colour and half in another, work three-quarter and quarter cross stitches (see p.105). Work the facial features and outlining in back stitch.

Press the completed work on the reverse side using a hot iron setting (see p.106), then mount the Christmas card following the instructions given on p.106.

Chick Gift Tag

This cheerful chick design is quick and easy to stitch, and is the perfect addition to a gift wrapped present for a baby. It can then be placed in a small frame if desired.

Measurements
The actual cross stitch design measures
2.5 x 3.5cm (1 x 1½in)

Materials
• Piece of cream 14-count aida fabric measuring
11.5 x 10cm (4½ x 4in)
• DMC or Anchor stranded embroidery cotton,
one skein each of the following colours
• Tapestry needle, size 24
• Cream gift tag with oval opening measuring
3 x 6cm (1¼ x 2¼in)
• Piece of ribbon about 12.5 cm (5in) long and
6mm (⅜in) wide

To make up
Following the chart and beginning centrally (see p.104), work the design in cross stitch using two strands of embroidery thread. Each square represents one cross stitch. Where squares are shown divided diagonally, with half in one colour and half in another, work three-quarter cross stitches (see p.105).

Press the completed work on the reverse side using a hot iron setting (see p.106), then mount the gift tag following the instructions given on p.106. Attach a small ribbon loop to the top left corner for hanging the tag on the present.

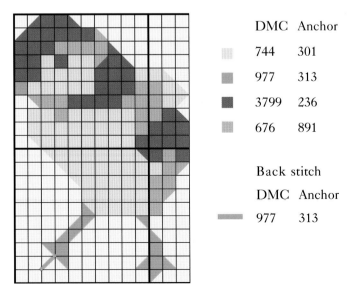

	DMC	Anchor
	744	301
	977	313
	3799	236
	676	891

Back stitch

	DMC	Anchor
	977	313

Baby Gift Tag

A present for a baby can be given an extra special finishing touch with this pretty gift tag. Afterwards, the gift tag is sure to be treasured as a keepsake.

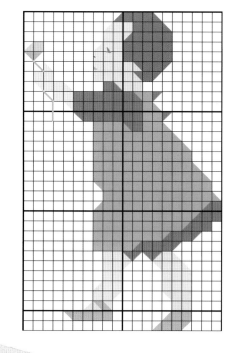

Measurements

The actual cross stitch design measures
4.5 x 2.5cm (1¾ x 1in)

Materials

• Piece of white 18-count aida fabric measuring
11.5 x 10cm (4 x 4½in)
• DMC or Anchor stranded embroidery cotton,
one skein each of the colours shown in the chart
• Tapestry needle, size 26
• Card with rectangular opening measuring
3 x 5.5cm (1¼ x 2⅛in)
• Piece of ribbon about 12.5 cm (5in) long and
6mm (⅜in) wide

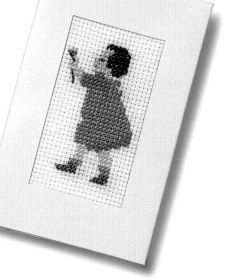

To make up

Following the chart and beginning centrally (see
p.104), work the design in cross stitch using two
strands of embroidery thread. Each square represents one cross stitch. Where squares are shown
divided diagonally, with half the square in one
colour and half in another, work three-quarter
cross stitches (see p.105). Work the facial features
in back stitch.

Press the completed work on the reverse side
using a hot iron setting (see p.106), then mount
the card following the instructions given on
p.106. Attach a small ribbon loop to the top left
corner for hanging the tag on the present.

DMC	Anchor
340	118
502	877
3752	976
839	360
948	778
743	305
3727	969

Back stitch

DMC	Anchor
502	877

PICTURES

Pictures

Colourful pictures on the nursery walls will make the room a pleasure to be in as well as stimulating the baby's imagination. There are ten pictures in this chapter, including one sampler worked simply and quickly on 14-count aida. I have varied the stitching fabric to try to cater for all tastes and, except for the Fairy Baby picture and the two angel pictures, all are quick to make up. Six are worked on 28-count evenweave fabric over two fabric threads each way, two

on 18-count aida and two on 14-count aida. If you prefer to work on aida rather than evenweave fabric, you can do so. The evenweave fabrics are all 28-count over two fabric threads each way which is the equivalent of 14-aida, so the designs will work out the same size. If you prefer to use 11-count aida the design will work out even larger, and you will need to use three strands of embroidery thread for good coverage. The 18-count designs can also be worked on 16- or 14-count aida.

The Fairy Baby picture is worked in DMC flower thread, which is a non-shiny cotton that comes in a single strand. It illustrates the delightful quote from J.M. Barrie's *The Little White Bird*. I have always loved fairies, and secretly thought how lovely it would be if they were real. However, recently, two friends of mine, who do not know each other and who are both perfectly sane individuals, have told me that they have seen them, one when she was quite young, and the other recently in the shrubbery in my garden. Both said that these fairies were much larger than they would have expected them to be, at least 1m (2¼ft) high, one with feathered wings and the other with wings made up of bands of shimmering light. I am still not entirely convinced, but am willing to be, and look hopefully in my shrubbery some evenings.

Angels and cherubs are more of my favourite things. The angel pictures I adapted from designs on the head and end board of a Victorian cot I found some years ago in an antique shop. The sides and base are long lost, but the ends serve as cupboard doors in my house. The pictures have a number of half stitches and are fairly time con-suming to make, but well worth the effort, and look lovely framed as a matching pair. They are worked on fawn evenweave fabric.

The little girl sitting on the steps nursing her dolls is worked on grey, 18-count aida. My inspi-ration came from an engraving in an old, children's book. This is quite a fiddly design to work, as there are a lot of half stitches on a small-count fabric. It can also be worked on 14-count fabric; it

will come up slightly larger, but be easier on the eyes to stitch.

There are two designs featuring children in bed. One, of a little girl sitting up in bed surrounded by her toys, is worked on cream, 28-count, evenweave fabric, and the other, of a little girl fast asleep clutching her teddy, is worked on pink, 28-count evenweave fabric.

The little girl leading the calf, holding some buttercups plucked from the field, is one of my favourites. The blue, 28-count, evenweave fabric serves as the sky, as it does in the Girl at the Window picture, where the little girl is releasing a small bird that has flown into her bedroom.

Fairy Baby Picture

"When the first baby laughed for the first time, its laugh broke into a thousand pieces and they all went skipping about, and that was the beginning of fairies."

Quotation from *"The Little White Bird"*, Sir J.M. Barrie.

Measurements
The actual cross stitch design measures
19 x 17cm (7½ x 6¾in)

Materials
• Piece of dark blue 18-count aida fabric measuring 35.5 x 35.5cm (14 x 14in)

• DMC Flower or Anchor Nordin embroidery threads , one skein each of the different colours shown in the chart
• Tapestry needle, size 26
• Piece of acid-free mounting board measuring 21 x 19cm (8¼ x 7½in)
• Strong thread for lacing

To make up
Following the chart and beginning centrally (see p.104), work the design in cross stitch using the flower embroidery threads. Each square represents one cross stitch. When all the cross stitching is complete, add the outlining on the baby's legs, arms and body in back stitch using a single strand of dark grey flower embroidery thread. Use the same colour of flower embroidery thread to back stitch the baby's eyes and nostrils, and also to indicate the outlines of the outer and inner ear.

Press the completed work on the reverse using a hot iron setting (see p.106). To finish the picture, either stretch it over stiff, acid-free mounting board (see p.106), or take it to a picture framer to be professionally stretched and framed.

DMC	Anchor		DMC	Anchor		DMC	Anchor		DMC	Anchor		Back stitch	
background			blanc	2		2933	975		2222	969		DMC	Anchor
ecru	387		2359	118		2924	851		2358	117		2773	392
2948	778		2950	4146		2766	324					2926	849
2415	398		2926	849		2327	972						
2579	852		2927	850		2346	47						

Baby in a Crib

This charming picture would make an ideal gift to celebrate a new born baby and is sure to be treasured for many years to come.

Measurements
The actual cross stitch design measures
17.75 x 10.75cm (7 x 4¼in)

Materials
• Piece of pale blue 28-count evenweave fabric
measuring 30.5 x 24cm (12 x 9½in)
• DMC or Anchor stranded embroidery cotton,
one skein each of the colours shown in the chart

• Tapestry needle, size 26
• Piece of acid-free mounting board to fit inside
your chosen frame
• Strong thread for lacing
• Picture frame

To make up
Following the chart and beginning centrally (see
p.104), work the design in cross stitch using two

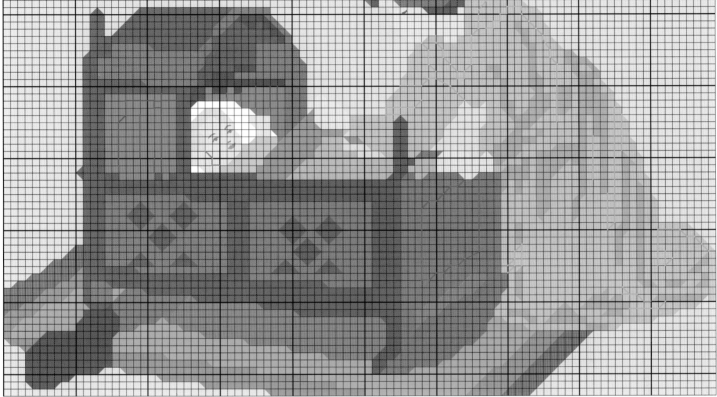
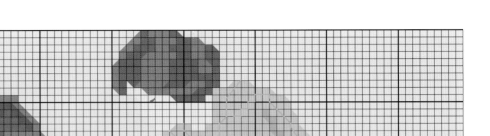

strands of embroidery thread. Each square represents one cross stitch over two threads of fabric each way. Where squares are shown divided diagonally, with half the square in one colour and half in another, work three-quarter cross stitches (see p.105). When cross stitching is complete, back stitch the outlining and features. Work the baby's eyes in French knots using deep blue thread.

Press the completed work on the reverse using a hot iron setting (see p.106). To finish, either stretch the embroidery over stiff, acid-free mounting board (see p.106), or take it to a picture framer to be professionally framed.

DMC	Anchor
3787	393
3021	905
3790	903
793	176
791	178
356	5976
3778	9575
3042	870
3041	871

DMC	Anchor
316	969
3731	38
778	968
blanc	1
3766	167
3774	778
355	341
3799	236
677	300

Back stitch	
DMC	Anchor
3021	905
3787	393
791	178
3041	871
778	968
793	176

Girl at a Window

A little girl releases a bird that has flown into her bedroom in this decorative cross stitched picture, which is worked in soft, pretty colours.

Measurements
The actual design measures 10.25 x 13.75cm (4⅛ x 5⅜in)

Materials
- Piece of light blue 14-count aida fabric measuring 23 x 29cm (9 x 11½in)
- DMC or Anchor stranded embroidery cotton, one skein each of the colours shown in the chart
- Tapestry needle, size 24
- Piece of acid-free mounting board
- Strong thread for lacing
- Picture frame

To make up
Following the chart and beginning centrally (see p.104), work the design in cross stitch using two strands of thread. Each square represents one cross stitch. Where squares are shown divided diagonally, with half the square in one colour and half in another, work three-quarter cross stitches (p.105). When all the cross stitching is complete, add the facial features and outlining in back stitch. The birds in the distance and the light, upper branches of the trees are also worked in back stitch using brown and green threads.

Press the completed work on the reverse using a hot iron setting (see p.106). To finish the picture, either stretch it over stiff, acid-free mounting board (see p.106), or take it to a picture framer to be professionally stretched and framed.

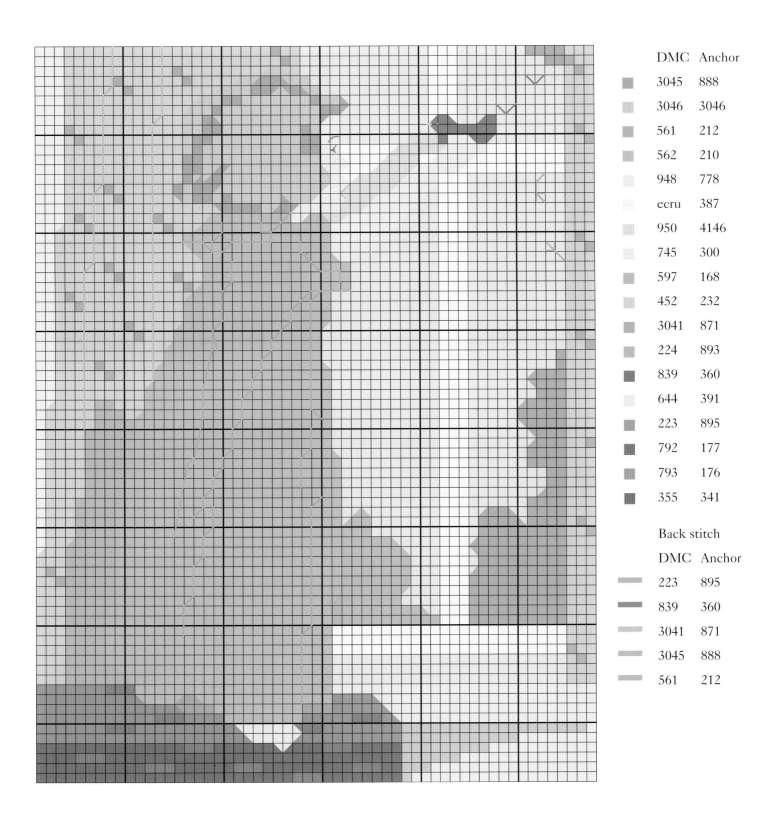

DMC	Anchor
3045	888
3046	3046
561	212
562	210
948	778
ecru	387
950	4146
745	300
597	168
452	232
3041	871
224	893
839	360
644	391
223	895
792	177
793	176
355	341

Back stitch

DMC	Anchor
223	895
839	360
3041	871
3045	888
561	212

Rustic Scene

A colourful picture to brighten the wall of the nursery. The design has a wealth of pretty detail, with a textural effect and further definition created by stitching some individual blades of grass.

Measurements
The actual cross stitch design measures 12.75 x 11cm (5 x 4⅜in)

Materials
• Piece of pale blue 28-count evenweave fabric measuring 30.5 x 33cm (12 x 13in)
• DMC or Anchor stranded embroidery cotton, one skein each of the colours shown in the chart
• Tapestry needle, size 26
• Piece of acid-free mounting board
• Strong thread for lacing
• Picture frame

To make up
Following the chart and beginning centrally (see p.104), work the design in cross stitch using two strands of embroidery thread. Each square represents one cross stitch over two threads of fabric each way. Where the squares on the chart are shown divided diagonally, with half the square in one colour and half in another, work three-quarter cross stitches (see p.105). When all the cross stitching is complete, add the features of the girl and the calf that she is leading across a meadow in back stitch, then back stitch the outlining and the blades of grass.

Press the completed work on the reverse using a hot iron setting (p.106). To finish the picture, either stretch the embroidery yourself over stiff, acid-free mounting board (see p.106) and then mount it in a shop-bought frame, or take it to a picture framer to be professionally stretched and framed.

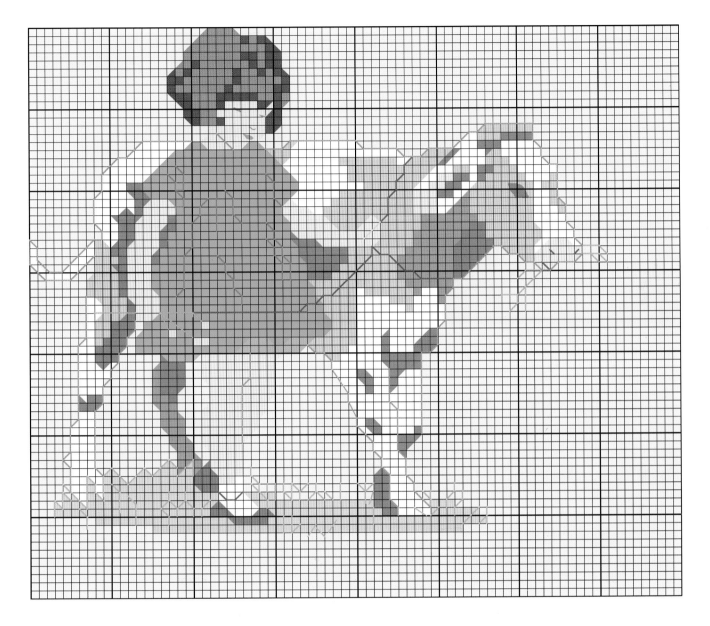

DMC	Anchor		DMC	Anchor		DMC	Anchor		Back stitch			Back stitch	
									DMC	Anchor		DMC	Anchor
3799	236		801	358		948	778		950	4146		3347	266
317	400		793	176		blanc	1		317	400		793	176
727	293		3809	169		223	895		3799	236			
434	365		597	168									
436	362		472	278									

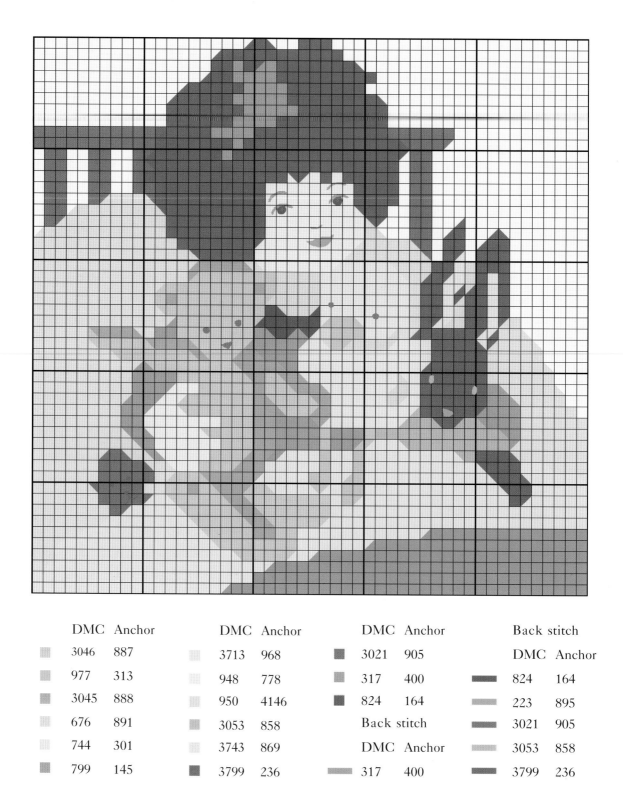

	DMC	Anchor		DMC	Anchor		DMC	Anchor	Back stitch		
	3046	887		3713	968		3021	905	DMC	Anchor	
	977	313		948	778		317	400	824	164	
	3045	888		950	4146		824	164	223	895	
	676	891		3053	858	Back stitch			3021	905	
	744	301		3743	869	DMC	Anchor		3053	858	
	799	145		3799	236	317	400		3799	236	

Girl in Bed with Toys

In this enchanting design, a girl sits up in bed with her favourite doll and cuddly toys. The vivid threads used to cross stitch the picture will add a welcome touch of colour to the nursery.

Measurements
The actual cross stitch design measures 9 x 9cm (3½ x 3 ½in)

Materials
• Piece of cream 28-count evenweave fabric measuring 20 x 20cm (8 x 8in)
• DMC or Anchor stranded embroidery cotton, one skein each of the colours shown in the chart
• Tapestry needle, size 26
• Strong thread for lacing
• Piece of acid-free mounting board
• Picture frame

To make up
Following the chart and beginning centrally (see p.104) work the design in cross stitch using two strands of embroidery thread. Each of the square represents one cross stitch over two fabric threads each way. Where squares are shown divided diagonally, with half the square in one colour and half in another, work three-quarter cross stitches (see p.105). When all the cross stitching is complete, add the features on the girl, chick, rabbit and puppy in back stitch.

Press the completed design on the reverse using a hot iron setting (see p.106). To finish the picture, either stretch the embroidery yourself over stiff, acid-free mounting board (see p.106), or take it to a picture framer to be professionally stretched and framed.

Child in Bed with a Teddy

The comforting image and warm colours of this picture make it an ideal decoration for a nursery, and it is sure to be a treasured piece in a child's room later on.

- DMC or Anchor stranded embroidery cotton, one skein each of the colours shown in the chart
- Tapestry needle, size 26
- Piece of acid-free mounting board to fit your chosen frame
- Strong thread for lacing
- Picture frame

To make up

Following the chart and beginning centrally (see p.104), work the design in cross stitch using two strands of embroidery thread. Each square represents one cross stitch over two fabric threads each way. Where squares are shown divided diagonally, with half the square in one colour and half in another, work three-quarter cross stitches (see p.105). When all the cross stitching is complete, add the features and outlining in back stitch. Work the eyes of the doll and toys in French knots.

Press the completed work on the reverse using a hot iron setting (see p.106). To finish the picture, either stretch the embroidery yourself over stiff, acid-free mounting board (see p.106), or take it to a picture framer to be professionally stretched and framed.

Measurements

The actual cross stitch design measures 13.5 x 9.5cm (5¼ x 3¾in)

Materials

- Piece of dusky pink 28-count evenweave fabric 25 x 28cm (10 x 11in)

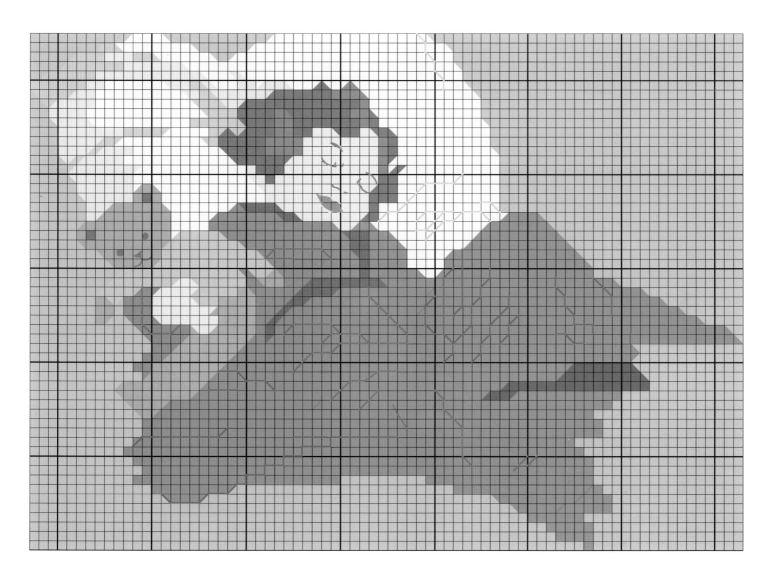

DMC	Anchor		DMC	Anchor		DMC	Anchor		Back stitch	
ecru	387		791	178		3042	870		DMC	Anchor
3033	830		3722	895		3045	888		791	178
3782	831		221	897		948	778		221	897
898	359		3021	905					3782	831
3807	177		3768	779					3021	905

Angels and Doves

This enchanting picture is worked in pretty, muted shades enlivened with touches of brilliant pink and would make a delightful gift.

Measurements
The actual cross stitch design measures
15.5 x 12.5cm (6 x 5in)

Materials
• Piece of fawn 28-count evenweave fabric
measuring 33 x 33cm (13 x 13in)
• DMC or Anchor stranded embroidery cotton,
one skein each of the colours shown in the chart
• Tapestry needle, size 26
• Sewing needle for embroidering features
• Piece of acid-free mounting board to fit inside
your chosen frame
• Strong thread for lacing
• Picture frame

To make up
Following the chart and beginning centrally (see
p.104), work the design in cross stitch using two
strands of embroidery thread. Each square represents one cross stitch worked over two threads of
evenweave fabric each way. Where squares are
shown divided diagonally, with half the square in
one colour and half in another colour, work three-
quarter cross stitches (see p.105). When all the
cross stitching is complete, add the outlining and
facial features in back stitch using a single strand
of embroidery thread.

Press the completed work on the reverse side
using a hot iron setting (see p.106). To finish the
picture, either stretch the embroidery yourself
over stiff, acid-free mounting board (see p.106)
and mount it in a shop-bought frame, or take it to
a picture framer to be professionally stretched
and framed.

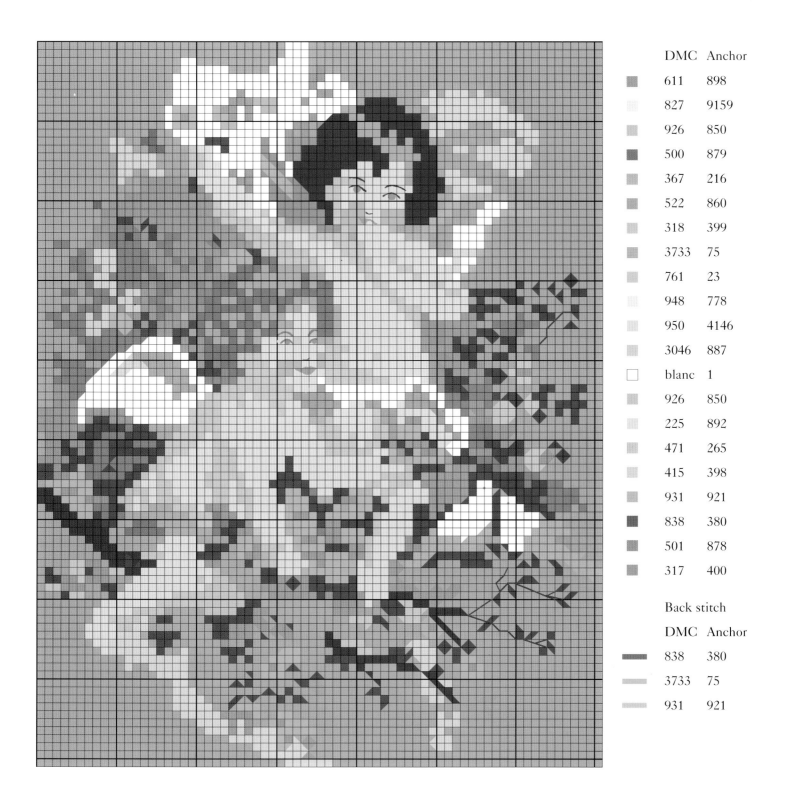

DMC	Anchor
611	898
827	9159
926	850
500	879
367	216
522	860
318	399
3733	75
761	23
948	778
950	4146
3046	887
blanc	1
926	850
225	892
471	265
415	398
931	921
838	380
501	878
317	400

Back stitch

DMC	Anchor
838	380
3733	75
931	921

Angels by a Stream

A delightful picture which would make a perfect pair with the Angels and Doves picture shown on the previous pages. The colours in this picture are softer and more subdued.

Measurements

The actual cross stitch design measures
12 x 15cm (4¾ x 6in)

Materials

• Piece of beige 28-count evenweave fabric, measuring 33 x 33cm (13 x 13in)
• DMC or Anchor stranded embroidery cotton, one skein each of the colours shown in the chart
• Tapestry needle, size 26
• Sewing needle for embroidering features
• Piece of acid-free mounting board to fit inside your chosen frame
• Strong thread for lacing
• Picture frame

To make up

Following the chart and beginning centrally (see p.104), work the design in cross stitch using two strands of thread. Each square represents one cross stitch over two threads of evenweave fabric each way. Where squares are shown divided diagonally, with half the square in one colour and half in another, work three-quarter cross stitches (see p.105).

Press the completed work on the reverse side using a hot iron setting (see p.106). To finish the picture, either stretch the embroidery yourself over stiff, acid-free mounting board (see p.106) and mount it in a shop-bought frame, or take it to a picture framer to be professionally stretched and framed.

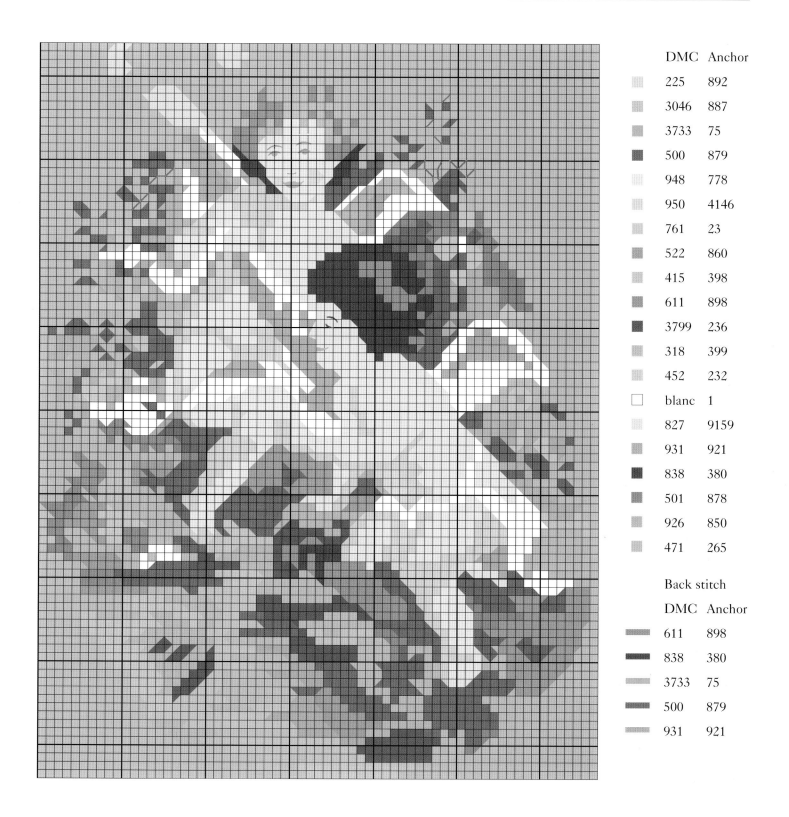

DMC	Anchor
225	892
3046	887
3733	75
500	879
948	778
950	4146
761	23
522	860
415	398
611	898
3799	236
318	399
452	232
blanc	1
827	9159
931	921
838	380
501	878
926	850
471	265

Back stitch

DMC	Anchor
611	898
838	380
3733	75
500	879
931	921

Girl on Steps

This charming picture is worked in a range of pretty, autumnal shades. When choosing a frame, ensure that its colour complements those of the embroidery.

Measurements

The actual cross stitch design measures 11.5 x 11cm (4½ x 4⅜in)

Materials

• Piece of grey 18-count aida fabric measuring 25 x 25cm (10 x 10in)
• DMC or Anchor stranded embroidery cotton, one skein each of the colours shown in the chart
• Tapestry needle, size 26
• Piece of acid-free mounting board
• Strong thread for lacing
• Picture frame

To make up

Following the chart and beginning centrally (see p.104), work the design in cross stitch using two strands of embroidery thread. Each square represents one cross stitch. Where squares are shown divided diagonally, with half of the square in one colour and half in another, work three-quarter cross stitches (see p.105). When all the cross stitching is complete, add the outlining on the girl, and the facial features of the girl and the doll in the pink dress, in back stitch.

Press the completed work on the reverse side using a hot iron setting (see p.106). To finish the picture, either stretch the embroidery yourself over stiff, acid-free mounting board (see p.106) and mount it in a shop-bought frame, or take it to a picture framer to be professionally stretched and framed.

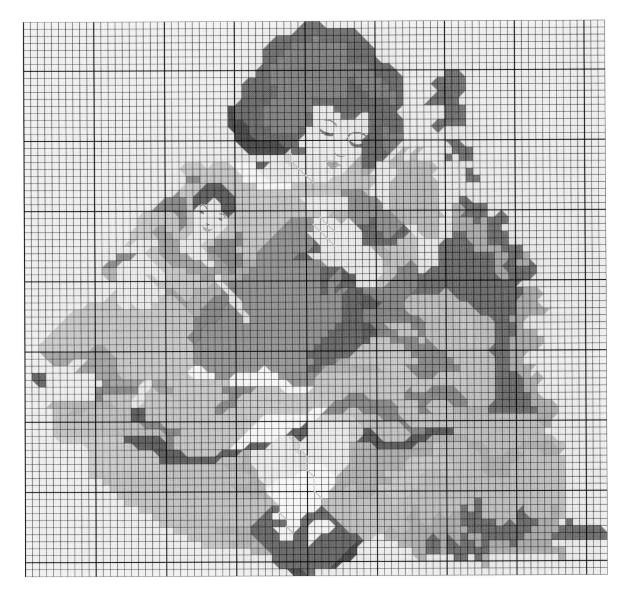

	DMC	Anchor		DMC	Anchor		DMC	Anchor		DMC	Anchor		Back stitch	
	3042	870		792	177		ecru	387		610	889		DMC	Anchor
	3740	872		948	778		3021	905		729	1		223	236
	760	9		950	4146		647	8581		3799	236		839	360
	761	23		367	216		415	398		838	380		3041	871
	793	176		500	879		414	235					647	8581
													3021	905

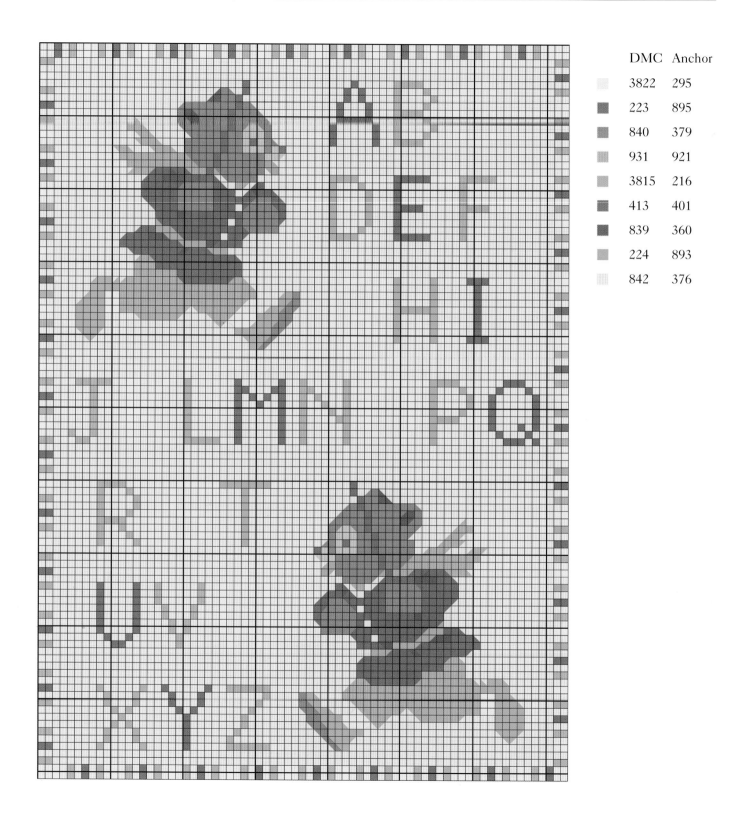

DMC	Anchor
3822	295
223	895
840	379
931	921
3815	216
413	401
839	360
224	893
842	376

Bear Sampler

Samplers look wonderfully in keeping with the tranquil setting of the nursery and this one, adorned with appealing bears, is certain to be popular.

Measurements

The actual cross stitch design measures 13.25 x 18.75cm (5¼ x 7⅜in)

Materials

• Piece of pink 14-count aida fabric measuring 28 x 34cm (11 x 13½in)
• DMC or Anchor stranded embroidery cotton, one skein each of the colours shown in the chart
• Tapestry needle, size 24
• Piece of acid-free mounting board to fit your chosen frame
• Strong thread for lacing
• Picture frame

To make up

Following the chart and beginning centrally (see p.104), work the design in cross stitch using two strands of embroidery cotton. Each square represents one cross stitch. Where squares are shown divided diagonally, with half of the square in one colour and half in another, work three-quarter cross stitches (see p.105). When all the cross stitching is complete, add the outlining and facial features in back stitch.

Press the completed work on the reverse side using a hot iron setting (see p.106). To finish the picture, either stretch the embroidery yourself over stiff, acid-free mounting board (see p.106) and mount it in a shop-bought frame, or take it to a picture framer to be professionally stretched and framed.

CLOTHING

Clothing

In this chapter you will discover a range of ways to transform a shop bought item of clothing quickly and easily into something individual and special. There are bib patterns made from 28-count evenweave with a winceyette backing for absorbency. The designs can be stitched on to a bought bib too, using waste canvas and edged with ribbon, bias tape and lace, if you would prefer not to make your own.

All the remaining items in this chapter, with the exception of the Mice Dungarees have the designs cross stitched directly on to the articles of clothing using waste canvas. The Mice Dungarees have a pocket decorated with a design of gardening mice stitched on to 28-count evenweave fabric, which is then sewn on to the bib of the dungarees. Any of the other designs can be made up in the same way if you prefer this method to using waste canvas.

The simplest of all the designs in this chapter, and one which is extremely effective, is the penguin motif stitched on to the little white sun hat. This has been designed for a little boy but would look equally appealing on a girl. The little girl's sun bonnet has a design of two scurrying chicks, one on each side.

All the designs are interchangeable, so don't feel that you should make each one on the particular type of clothing shown in the book. Designs from any of the other chapters can also be used – for instance, the chick from the Cards and Gift Tags chapter would look charming on a T-shirt or sleepsuit

and the teddy design from the sleepsuit could be stitched as a card or
gift tag, or repeated as a border along the edge of a curtain or towel.

Cotton T-shirts are a very handy item of clothing and I have
included two in the chapter, one with a lion and child, and the other
with a tiger and child. The design ideas come from a magazine cut-
out I found in a scrapbook I was given when an elderly neighbour of
mine died some years ago. She had filled it as a child with the most
delightful scraps, some of them Victorian. There are more animals from
this scrapbook that I look forward to adapting for cross stitch designs in
future books.

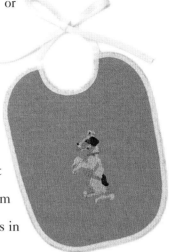

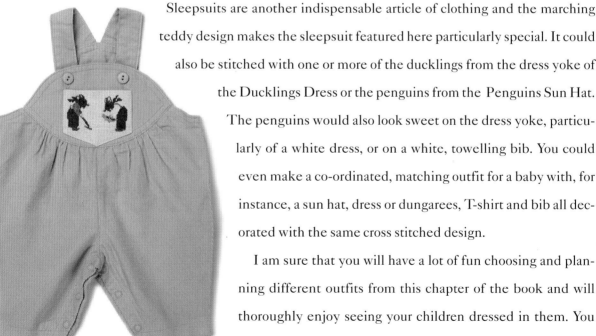

Sleepsuits are another indispensable article of clothing and the marching
teddy design makes the sleepsuit featured here particularly special. It could
also be stitched with one or more of the ducklings from the dress yoke of
the Ducklings Dress or the penguins from the Penguins Sun Hat.
The penguins would also look sweet on the dress yoke, particularly of a white dress, or on a white, towelling bib. You could
even make a co-ordinated, matching outfit for a baby with, for
instance, a sun hat, dress or dungarees, T-shirt and bib all decorated with the same cross stitched design.

I am sure that you will have a lot of fun choosing and planning different outfits from this chapter of the book and will
thoroughly enjoy seeing your children dressed in them. You
can feel proud, too, when family and friends admire the
clothes that your baby is wearing and you tell them that you stitched
the embroidered designs yourself.

Kitten Bib

This bib with its cheerful and friendly kitten in a pretty green smock will brighten up every tea time.

Measurements

The actual design measures 3.5 x 7.5cm
(1⅓ x 3in)

Materials

• Piece of lilac 28- count evenweave fabric
measuring 25.5 x 25cm (10 x 8in)
• DMC or Anchor stranded
embroidery cotton, one skein
each of the colours that are shown
in the chart
• Tapestry needle, size 24
• Piece of white towelling or winceyette
measuring 20 x 25.5 cm (10 x 8in)
• Length of 1.25 (½in) wide cream bias
binding measuring 1.4m (55in)
• Cream sewing thread
• Piece of paper from which to cut the
pattern

To make up

Centre the design on the fabric (see p.104).
Following the chart and beginning centrally
(see p.104), work the design in cross stitch
using two strands of thread. Each square
represents one cross stitch. Where squares are
shown divided diagonally, with half the square in
one colour and half in another, work three-
quarter cross stitches (see p. 105). Work the
outlining in back stitch, and the facial features in
back and satin stitch.

Press the completed design on the reverse side

using a hot iron setting (see p.106). To finish
make up the bib following the instructions given
on p.108.

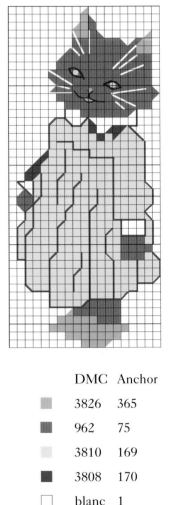

	DMC	Anchor
	3826	365
	962	75
	3810	169
	3808	170
	blanc	1

Back stitch

	DMC	Anchor
	3808	170
	blanc	1

Dog Bib

A dog begging for food makes a delightful motif on this bib, which will ensure that every meal becomes a special occasion.

Measurements

The actual cross stitch design measures
4 x 8cm (1¾ x 3¼in)

Materials

- Piece of blue 28-count evenweave fabric measuring 25.5 x 20 cm (10 x 8in)
- DMC or Anchor stranded embroidery cotton, one skein each of the colours shown in the chart
- Tapestry needle, size 26
- Piece of white towelling or winceyette measuring 20 x 25.5cm (8 x 10in)
- Length of 1.25cm (½in) wide white bias binding measuring 1.4m (55in)
- White sewing thread
- Sewing needle
- Piece of paper from which to cut the pattern

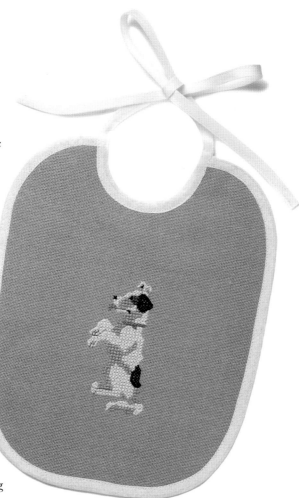

To make up

Centre the design on the fabric (see p.104). Following the chart and beginning centrally (see p.104), work the design in cross stitch using two strands of embroidery thread in the needle. Each square represents one cross stitch worked over two fabric threads each way. Where squares are shown divided diagonally, with one half in one colour and half in another, work three-quarter cross stitches (see p. 105).

Press the completed work on the reverse using a hot iron setting (see p.106), then make up the bib following the instructions given on p.108.

	DMC	Anchor
	415	398
	317	262
	793	260
	3688	66
	3799	236
☐	blanc	1

Back stitch

	DMC	Anchor
	3799	236
	317	400

Mice Dungarees

One mouse with a rake and another with a trug add a lively and rustic style to a pair of dungarees, transforming them into an extra special item of clothing.

Measurements
Each actual design measures 3.5 x 4.75cm
(1⅜ x 1⅞in)

Materials
• Dungarees
• Piece of 28-count evenweave fabric measuring 15 x 15cm (6 x 6in)
• DMC or Anchor stranded embroidery cotton, one skein each of the colours in the chart
  • Tapestry needle, size 26
    • Sewing thread and needle

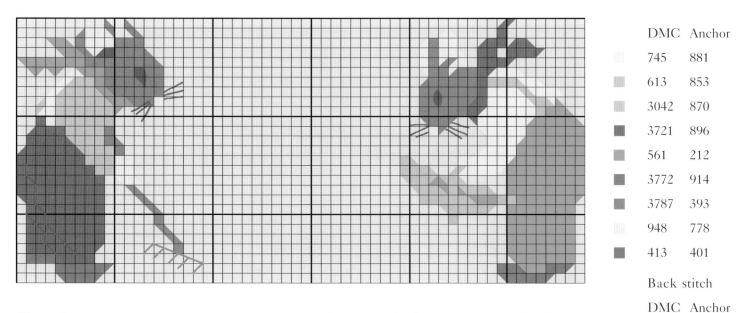

DMC	Anchor
745	881
613	853
3042	870
3721	896
561	212
3772	914
3787	393
948	778
413	401

Back stitch

DMC	Anchor
413	401
221	897
3787	393

To make up

Centre the design on the fabric for the pocket.

Following the chart and beginning centrally (see p.104), work the design in cross stitch using two strands of thread. Each square represents one cross stitch over two threads of fabric each way. When all the cross stitching is complete, add the eyes and whiskers in back stitch.

Press the completed work on the reverse using a hot iron setting (see p.106).

Cut out the fabric to the shape required for the pocket – generally a square or a rectangle – allowing a 1.5cm (½in) seam allowance at the sides and lower edge, and a 2cm (¾in) seam allowance on the upper edge. Press under the seam allowances all round, folding the fabric over twice at the top edge, then tack the pocket in place on the garment. Machine or back stitch around the sides and lower edge of the pocket through all fabric layers about 6mm (¼in) in from the edge.

Teddy Sleepsuit

A *baby will be happy curling up to go to sleep in a sleepsuit adorned with this delightful teddy bear motif.*

Measurements

The actual cross stitch design measures 7 x 4cm (2¾ x 1⅜in)

Materials

- Sleepsuit
- Piece of 12-count waste canvas measuring 10 x 10cm (4 x 4in)
- DMC or Anchor stranded embroidery cotton, one skein each of the colours in the chart
- Tapestry needle, size 26

To make up

Stitch the waste canvas into position on the left side of the sleepsuit with the top edge 6.5cm (2½in) down from top. Centre the design on the canvas (see p.104).

Following the chart and beginning centrally, work the design in cross stitch using three strands of embroidery thread, Each square represents

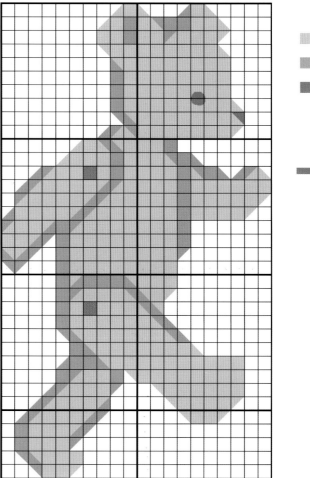

	DMC	Anchor
	3046	887
	3045	888
	839	360

Back stitch

	DMC	Anchor
	413	401

one cross stitch. When all the cross stitching is complete, embroider the eye, and the nose with the dark grey embroidery thread. Remove the waste canvas by moistening it and pulling out the horizontal, and then the vertical, threads one at a time (see p.102). Always remember to rinse the project thoroughly afterwards to make sure that any starch from the waste canvas is removed from the fabric.

Ducklings Dress

Decorate a dress yoke with this enchanting design worked in shades of cheerful yellow.

Measurements

The design measures 9 x 5 cm (3½ x 2 in)

Materials

- Plain dress with yoke
- Piece of waste canvas measuring 11 x 9cm (4⅓ x 3½in)
- DMC or Anchor stranded embroidery cotton, one skein each of the colours shown in the chart
- Tapestry needle, size 26
- Tweezers
- Sewing needle and thread

To make up

Sew the waste canvas in position on the dress yoke. Now centre the design on the waste canvas (see p.104).

Following the chart and beginning centrally (see p.104), work the design in cross stitch using two strands of embroidery thread. Each square represents one cross stitch. Where squares are shown divided diagonally, with half of the square in one colour and half in another, work three-quarter cross stitches (see p.105). When all the cross stitching is complete, work the eye in French knots using very dark brown thread. Remove the waste canvas by moistening it, then pulling out the threads one at a time (see p. 102).

Press on the wrong side using an iron setting appropriate for the fabric.

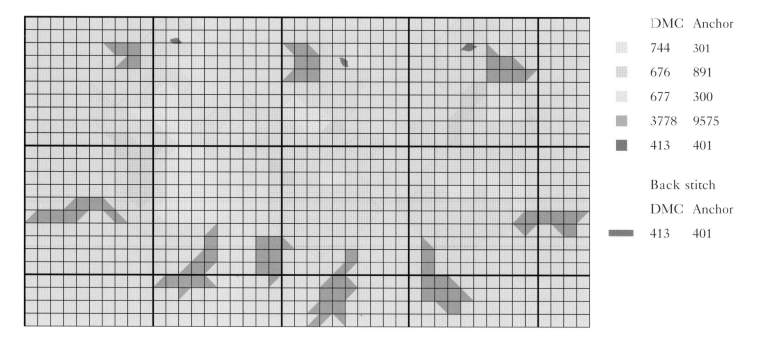

	DMC	Anchor
	744	301
	676	891
	677	300
	3778	9575
	413	401

Back stitch

	DMC	Anchor
	413	401

Lion and Child T-Shirt

Brighten up a plain T-shirt for a baby with this fun and colourful cross stitch design and it is certain to become a firm favourite.

Measurements

The actual cross stitch design measures 8 x 6cm (3¼ x 2½in)

Materials

• T-shirt
• Piece of waste canvas measuring 11 x 10cm (4⅓ x 4in)
• DMC or Anchor stranded embroidery cotton, one skein each of the colours shown in the chart
• Tapestry needle, size 24
• Sewing needle and thread

To make up

Position the waste canvas on the front of the T-shirt and tack around the edges to hold it in place. Centre the design on the canvas (see p.104).

Following the chart and beginning centrally (see p.104), work the design in cross stitch using two strands of embroidery thread. Each square represents one cross stitch. When all the cross stitching is complete, add the lion's facial features in back stitch and work the eyes in French knots using brown embroidery thread.

Remove the waste canvas following the instructions given on p.102. Press the T-shirt on the wrong side using an iron setting appropriate for the fabric (see p.106).

	DMC	Anchor
	3047	886
	340	118
	898	683
	3688	66
	948	778
	3816	221
	422	943

Back stitch

	DMC	Anchor
	898	359

Tiger and Child T-Shirt

This decorative cross stitched motif is an ideal way to jazz up a plain T-shirt. You could also use your own combination of shades to complement a different T-shirt colour.

Measurements

The actual design measures 7.5 x 7.5cm (3 x 3in)

Materials

• T-shirt

• Piece of waste canvas measuring 11.5 x 11.5cm (4½ x 4½in)

• DMC or Anchor stranded embroidery cotton, one skein each of the colours shown in the chart

• Tapestry needle, size 24

• Sewing needle and thread

To make up

Position the waste canvas on the front of the T-shirt and tack around the edges. Centre the design on the canvas (see p.102).

Following the chart, work the design in cross stitch using two strands of embroidery thread. Each square represents one cross stitch. When stitching is complete, add the child's facial features and the outlining on the tiger in back stitch.

Remove the waste canvas (see p.102). Press the T-shirt on the wrong side using an iron setting appropriate for the fabric (see p.106).

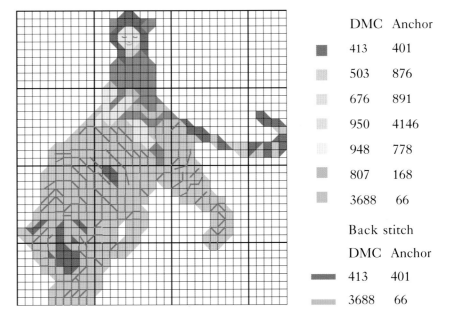

	DMC	Anchor
■	413	401
	503	876
	676	891
	950	4146
	948	778
■	807	168
■	3688	66

Back stitch

	DMC	Anchor
—	413	401
—	3688	66

Chick Bonnet

Decorate a baby's bonnet with a cheerful design of cross stitched chicks. The bonnet will keep a baby warm while bringing a touch of springtime to any day of the year.

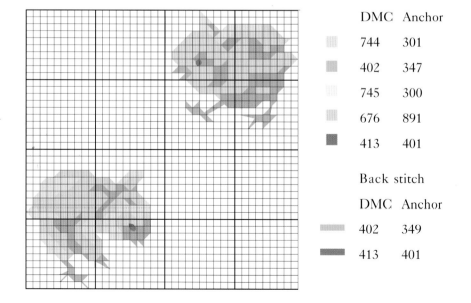

Measurements

The actual cross stitch design measures 3 x 3cm (1⅜ x 1⅜in)

Materials

• DMC or Anchor stranded embroidery cotton, one skein each of the colours shown in the chart
• Piece of waste canvas measuring 5 x 5cm (2 x 2in)
• Tapestry needle, size 26
• Sewing needle and thread

To make up

Stitch the piece of waste canvas into the desired position on the bonnet following the instructions given for working with waste canvas on p.102. Following the chart and beginning centrally (see p.104), work the design in cross stitch using two strands of embroidery thread. Where squares are shown divided diagonally, with half the square in one colour and half in another, work three-quarter cross and quarter cross stitches. When all the cross stitching is complete, remove the waste canvas (see p.102), and work the eyes in French knots using the dark grey thread.

Press on the wrong side using an iron setting appropriate for the fabric (see p.102).

	DMC	Anchor
	744	301
	402	347
	745	300
	676	891
	413	401

Back stitch

	DMC	Anchor
	402	349
	413	401

Penguins Sun Hat

A sun hat is vital for protecting a baby's head in hot weather so why not make it really decorative with a cross stitch design of beguiling penguins.

Measurements
The actual design measures 5 x 4.25cm
(2 x 1¾in)

Materials
• Sun hat
• Piece of waste canvas measuring 9 x 6.5cm
(3½ x 2½in)
• DMC or Anchor stranded embroidery cotton, one skein each of the colours shown in the chart
• Tapestry needle, size 26
• Needle and sewing thread

To make up
Position the waste canvas at the centre front with the lower edge on the seam of the brim and stitch in place. Centre the design on the canvas (see p.104).

Following the chart and beginning centrally (see p.104), work the design in cross stitch using two strands of embroidery thread. Each square represents one cross stitch. When all the cross stitching is complete, add the outlining and features in back stitch. Work the eyes in French knots using the dusty pink thread that was also used for cross stitching the beaks and feet.

Remove the waste canvas by moistening it and pulling out the horizontal, and then the vertical, threads one at a time (see p.102).

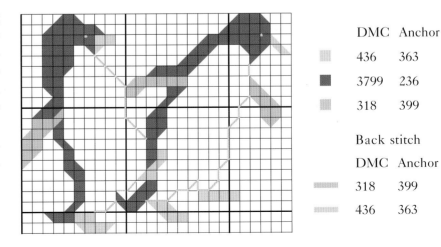

	DMC	Anchor
	436	363
	3799	236
	318	399

Back stitch

	DMC	Anchor
	318	399
	436	363

THE NURSERY

The Nursery

A complete, individual look can be created for your baby's room by making the items in this chapter. The colours of the designs have been co-ordinated so that they match and complement one another. I have chosen cream as the linking colour, mixed with lilac and pale blue. However, if you prefer, you can use your imagination to create the colour scheme of your choice to blend in with the general colours of the room. Articles could be made up in pink and cream, or in blue and pink, or all in cream. Alternatively, you could make everything in the purest white. Planning the colour scheme is part of the fun.

If you like cross stitching but do not like actually making up the items, you can always buy sheets, plain cushion covers and so on, then stitch the designs on to them using waste canvas as in the clothes chapter or, if the designs are small enough, you can use aida band as a border along the top of, say, a sheet or towel. For example, the rabbit design on the towel could be used to create a complete matching set as a border on a sheet, on a cushion, along the edge of a laundry bag, and even as a curtain tie back and to decorate a cotton wool bag.

This chapter includes designs for a crib cover and sheet for a new born baby. The cover is in pale blue and the sheet is in cream with a lace edging, and both are designed to fit either a crib or moses basket. A matching lace-edged cushion, adorned with a cross stitched design of lilac and blue frocked mice, completes this lovely set. The cushion can be used either to prop up the baby slightly in the crib when awake or on a nursery chair. In addition, there is a pattern for a cot cover and matching cot bumper in lilac, decorated with a rabbit design. There is also a cream, rabbit cushion, this time made up with a cord edging. These designs are all stitched on 28-count, evenweave fabric.

Also stitched on to aida band is the design of rabbits which forms a border on a cream towel. The ducklings or chicks from the clothing chapter would look lovely stitched on to a towel in this way too, or a row of the gift tag chick repeated along the length of the band would be effective. Work out the positions of any design you choose first so that the motifs are positioned evenly along the length of the border.

On the following pages, there is also a roomy, double thickness calico bag that can be used either as a handy place to store a collection of small toys to avoid clutter, or as a carry-all to take on outings and holidays. Decorating it is a charming design of a child pushing her doll along in a wheelbarrow. This has been stitched on to the calico with waste canvas.

A useful laundry bag completes the items in this chapter. It can be hung near the changing mat ready to stuff all those wet and dirty vests and sleepsuits into. It is stitched directly on to cream 28-count and pale blue, evenweave fabrics, but could be made up in any material with the design sewn on to waste canvas. It could also be used as a shoebag for an older child, or even for an adult.

Mice Laundry Bag

One mouse presents another with a bouquet of flowers in the design for this appealing laundry bag, which has a practical, drawstring opening.

Measurements

The actual design meaures 18.25cm x 11.5cm (7¼ x 4½in)

The bag measures 39.5 x 54.5cm (15½ x 21½in)

Materials

• Piece of cream 28-count evenweave fabric measuring 114 x 43cm (45 x 17in)
• Two pieces of pale blue 28 count evenweave fabric measuring 12.75 x 43cm (5 x 17in)
• Tapestry needle, size 26
• Length of 5mm (¼in) wide piping cord measuring 2m (2yd)
• Cream sewing thread
• Sewing needle

To make up

Fold the fabric in half as shown in the diagram on p.106. Position the design centrally so that the lower edge is 7.5cm (3in) up from the fold and the upper edge is 37cm (14½in) down from the top of the fabric.

Following the chart and beginning centrally (see p.104), work the design in cross stitch using two strands of embroidery thread. Each square represents one cross stitch over two threads of fabric. When all the cross stitching is complete, add the outlining on the mice and the flower stems in back stitch.

Press the completed work on the reverse using a hot iron setting (see p.106), then make up the bag following the instructions on p.106.

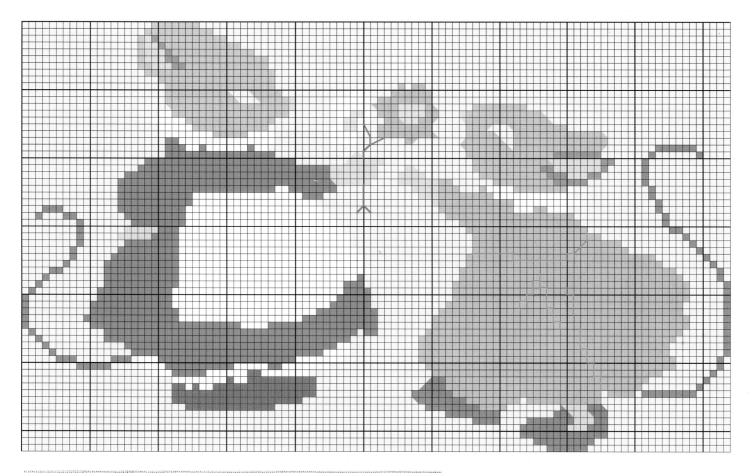

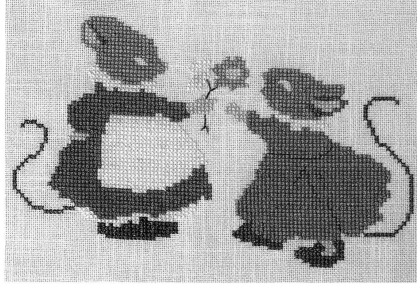

DMC	Anchor		DMC	Anchor
744	301		501	878
3790	236		646	8581
793	176		648	900
3774	778		3042	870
778	968		blanc	1

Back stitch

DMC	Anchor
501	878
3740	872

Mice Crib Set

This co-ordinating crib set of cushion, sheet and crib cover will look enchanting in the nursery. To decorate this set, mice in colourful frocks form a charming motif.

MICE CUSHION

Measurements

The actual design measures 13.5 x 7.5cm
(5¼ x 3in)
The cushion measures 35.5 x 35.5cm (14 x 14in)

Materials

•Two pieces of cream 28-count evenweave
fabric measuring 40.5 x 40.5cm (16 x 16in)
• DMC or Anchor stranded embroidery cotton,
one skein each of the colours shown in the chart
• Piece of 5cm (2in) wide cream lace 1.9m
(1¼ft) in length
• Cream sewing thread
• Cushion pad measuring 35.5cm (14in) square

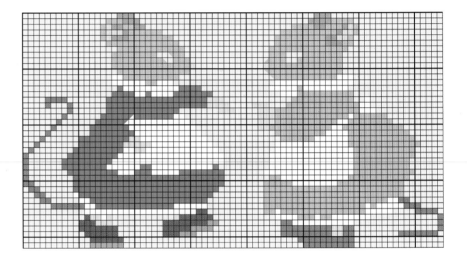

To make up

Centre the design on one of the fabric pieces.
Following the chart and beginning centrally (see
p.104), work the design in cross stitch using two
strands of embroidery thread. Each square represents one cross stitch worked over two threads of
fabric each way.

Press the completed design on the reverse
using a hot iron setting (see p.106), then make up
the cushion following the instructions below.

To make a lace-edged cushion

With right sides facing, pin and then tack lace to
the edges of the cushion front so that the stitching
line is 2.5cm (1in) in from the sides, gathering
corners so that the edge of the lace lies flat all
around the cushion. Join ends of lace together.
Machine or back stitch along the line of tacking.

	DMC	Anchor
	648	900
	3774	778
	646	8581
	blanc	1
	3790	236
	3042	68
	501	878
	793	176

Place the other piece of fabric on top, right sides together and, being careful not to catch the lace, tack and then stitch the two pieces of fabric together along the first line of stitching on three sides, leaving a gap on one side to insert the cushion pad. Clip corners and turn right side out. Insert the cushion pad and slipstitch to close gap.

MICE SHEET

Measurements

The blue frocked mouse measures 6.5 x 7.25cm (2½ x 2⅞in); the mauve frocked mouse measures 6 x 7.25cm (2⅜ x 2⅞in). From the start of the first pair of mice to the start of the second pair measures 16.5cm (6½in). (These measurements are for 28-count fabric only, the finished designs will be larger on the 12-count waste canvas.)
The sheet measures 99 x 145cm (39 x 57in)

Materials

• Piece of fabric measuring 103 x 149cm (40½ x 58½in)
• 28-count cream evenweave fabric measuring 102 x 76cm (40 x 30in), or cream cotton sheeting using a strip of waste canvas measuring approximately 99 x 11cm (39 x 4½in)
• Piece of cream 5cm (2in) wide lace, 1.1m (40in) in length
• DMC or Anchor stranded embroidery cotton, one skein each of the colours that are shown in the chart
• Tapestry needle, size 24
• Cream sewing thread

To make up

Position the lower edge of the mice design 6.5cm (2½in) up from the edge of the fabric. As the sheet tucks

around the side of the mattress – generally about 56cm (22in) in width – start the left side of the first mouse 23.5cm (9¼in) in from the left fabric edge. If preferred, the mice can be worked along the complete edge and positioned accordingly. If using waste canvas, you must also first work out the positions of the mice. It is often easier to begin by marking the design area with a line of tacking stitches These should start and finish 23.5cm (⅛in) in from the sides of the fabric and 6.5cm (2⅛in) up from the lower edge, or wherever you have decided to begin stitching.

	DMC	Anchor
■	648	900
▓	3774	778
■	646	8581
□	blanc	1
■	3790	903
▒	3042	870
■	501	878
■	793	176

Following the chart and beginning centrally (see p.104), work the design in cross stitch using two strands of embroidery thread. Each square represents one cross stitch worked over two fabric threads.

Press the completed work on the reverse using a hot iron setting (see p.106). Turn under a double 1cm (⅜in) hem around all four edges of the sheet and press in place. Attach lace along the line of hem stitching, below the row of mice.

MICE CRIB COVER

Measurements
The actual size of the design measures 17.5 x 11.75cm (6¾ x 4½in)
The cover measures 80 x 94cm (31½ x 37in)

Materials
• Piece of pale blue 28-count evenweave fabric measuring 85 x 99cm (33½ x 39in)
• DMC or Anchor stranded embroidery cotton, one skein each of the colours shown in the chart
• Tapestry needle, size 26
• Pale blue sewing thread

To make up
Centre the design on the fabric (see p.104). Following the chart and beginning centrally (see p.104), work the design in cross stitch using two strands of embroidery thread. Each square represents one cross stitch worked over two fabric threads each way.

Press the completed design on the reverse side using a hot iron setting (see p.106). Turn the edges under twice by 1cm (½in), tack and hem.

	DMC	Anchor
	648	900
	3774	778
	646	8581
	blanc	1
	798	131
	778	968
	501	878
	3790	903
	3042	870

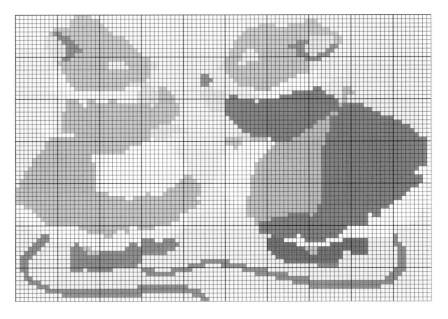

Toy Bag

This colourful toy bag will add a cheerful touch to the nursery. Storing toys in this way will help to keep floors and surfaces free of clutter too.

Measurements

The actual design measures 14 x 13.5cm (5¼ x 5½in)
The bag measures 49.5 x 34.25cm (19½ x 13½in)

Materials

- Piece of 142cm (56in) wide calico measuring 1m (1yd) used double
- Piece of cream 2.5cm (1in) wide seam or bias binding 3.25m (3½yd) in length
- DMC or Anchor stranded embroidery cotton, one skein of each of the colours shown in the chart
- Piece of cream ribbon 3.75cm (1½in) wide 2m (2¼yd) in length used double
- Piece of 12-count waste canvas measuring 20 x 20cm (8 x 8in)
- Cream sewing thread
- Sewing needle
- Pins
- Four buttons

To make up

Fold the fabric in half lengthwise. Measure 49.5cm (19½in) from the fold and cut – the two strips that are cut off should measure 21.5cm x 91.5cm (8½in x 36in). Tack the waste canvas on to the large, folded piece of fabric through both thicknesses with the lower edge 2.5cm (1in) up from the lower edge of the fabric and in the centre of the width. Centre the design on the fabric

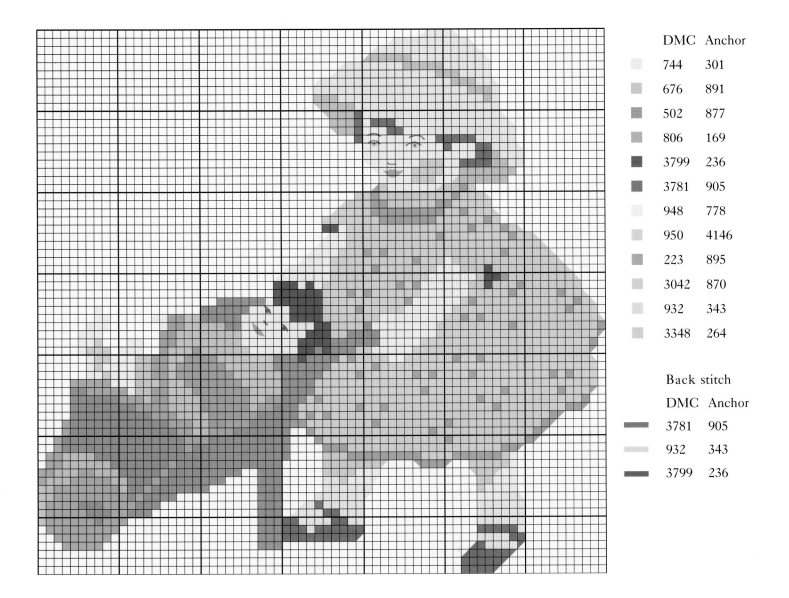

DMC	Anchor
744	301
676	891
502	877
806	169
3799	236
3781	905
948	778
950	4146
223	895
3042	870
932	343
3348	264

Back stitch

DMC	Anchor
3781	905
932	343
3799	236

(see p.104) and position it with the lower edge 6cm (2⅜in) up from the lower edge of the fabric.

Following the chart and beginning centrally (see p.104), work the design in cross stitch using two strands of embroidery thread. Each square represents one cross stitch. Remove the waste canvas from the completed design by moistening it and pulling out the horizontal, and then the vertical, threads one at a time (see p. 102). Work the facial features in back stitch. The little girl's eyes are worked in French knots using sky blue embroidery cotton. The doll's eyes are also worked in French knots using deep blue embroidery cotton.

Press the completed work on the reverse side using a hot iron setting (see p.106), then make up the Toy Bag following the instructions that are given on p. 107.

Rabbit Towel

Make bathtimes a special event by decorating a plain towel with a border featuring this attractive design of a pair of cheerful rabbits. While not in use the towel will brighten up the bathroom or nursery.

Measurements

The actual cross stitch design measures 9.5 x 4.5cm (3¾ x 1¾in)

Materials

• Piece of 15-count 5cm (2in) wide cream aida band, the width of your towel plus 2cm (½in) turn under for each side.

• DMC or Anchor stranded embroidery cotton, one skein each of the colours shown in the chart

• Tapestry needle, size 24

• Towel

• Cream sewing thread

To make up

Work out the positions of the pairs of rabbits so that they are evenly spaced along the length of the border. Following the chart and beginning centrally (see p.104), work the design in cross stitch using two strands of embroidery thread.

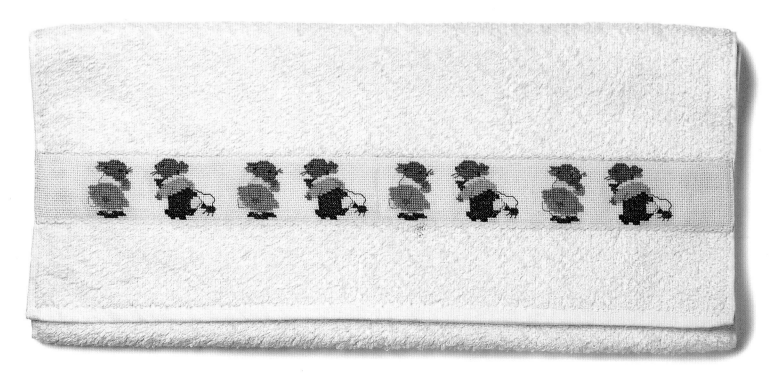

When all the cross stitching is complete, add the features and outlining in back stitch using one strand of embroidery thread in the colours shown in the chart.

Press the completed design on the reverse side using a hot iron setting (see p.106). Turn under the sides of the band, and machine stitch or back stitch it in position on the towel.

The idea of cross stitching a design on a wide aida band to form a border can be adapted in a variety of ways. For example, a cross stitched border could be stitched along the hems of a pair of otherwise plain nursery curtains, or used to decorate a tablecloth or fabric rug.

	DMC	Anchor		DMC	Anchor	Back stitch		
							DMC	Anchor
☐	blanc	1		501	878		3787	393
	642	392		3743	869		413	401
	3787	393		930	922		642	392
	224	893		413	401			
	3821	305		3721	896			

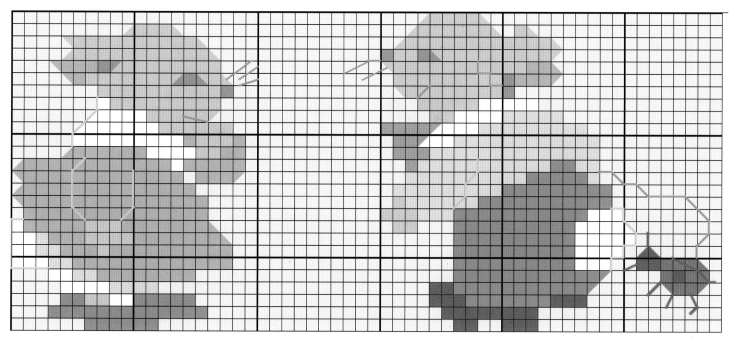

Rabbit Cot Set

A design featuring two pairs of irresistible, dancing rabbits adorns this pretty cot bumper and a complementary design of two rabbits taking a stroll together decorates a cot cover to complete the set. The set will add a perfect finishing touch to any nursery.

RABBIT COT BUMPER

Measurements
The actual cross stitch design measures 16 x 11cm (6¼ x 4⅛in)

Materials
• Three pieces of lilac 28-count evenweave fabric measuring 62 x 37cm (24½ x 14½in)
• Three pieces of backing fabric measuring 62 x 37cm (25 x 14½in) or more lilac evenweave
• Four pieces of heavyweight wadding measuring 58.5 x 30.5cm (23 x 12in)
• Two pieces of heavyweight wadding 56 x 30.5cm (22 x 12in)
(Cots vary in size so, to make sure the

bumper fits, measure halfway up the cot for the height, and halfway along one side and across the back for the width. Adjust the fabric and wadding measurements given here to fit your cot if this is necessary.)
• DMC or Anchor stranded embroidery cotton, one skein each of the colours shown in the chart
• Tapestry needle, size 26
• Length of 2.5cm (1in) wide cream cotton seam binding measuring 6.5m (7yd)
• Cream sewing thread
• Sewing needle

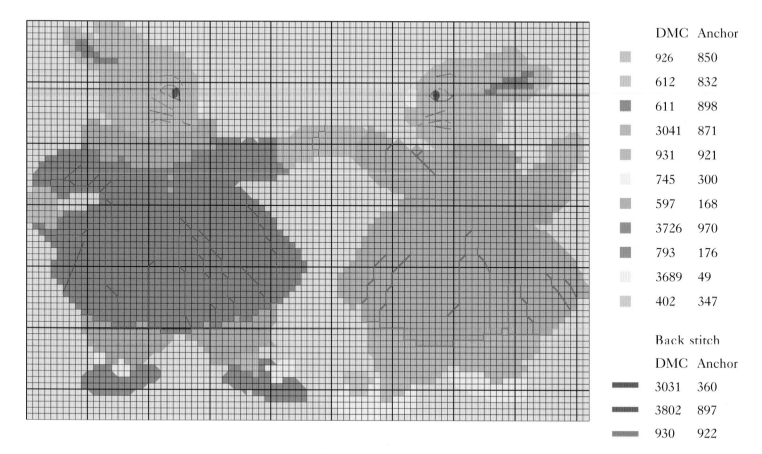

	DMC	Anchor
	926	850
	612	832
	611	898
	3041	871
	931	921
	745	300
	597	168
	3726	970
	793	176
	3689	49
	402	347

Back stitch

	DMC	Anchor
	3031	360
	3802	897
	930	922

To make up

For the back piece of the bumper, centre the design on the smaller piece of evenweave fabric. For the side pieces, find the centre of the larger fabric piece and position the two pairs of rabbits so that there is a 7.5cm (3in) gap between them or, if your cot size differs from the above, so that they are positioned equidistantly.

Following the chart and beginning centrally (see p.104), work the design in cross stitch using two strands of embroidery thread. Each square represents one cross stitch over two fabric threads. When all the cross stitching is complete, work the outlining and features in back stitch.

Press the completed work on the reverse using a hot iron setting (see p.106), then make up the bumper following the instructions on p.107

RABBIT COT COVER

Measurements

The actual cross stitch design measures 16 x 15cm (6¼ x 6in)
The cover measures 144 x 100cm (56½ x 39½in)

Materials

• Piece of lilac 28-count evenweave fabric measuring 144 x 100cm (56½ x 39½in)
• Length of 2.5cm (1in) wide cream cotton seam binding measuring 5m (5⅓yd)
• DMC or Anchor stranded embroidery cotton, one skein each of the colours that are shown in the chart
• Tapestry needle, size 26
• Cream sewing thread

To make up

Centre the design on the fabric (see p.104).

Following the chart and beginning centrally (see p. 104), work the design in cross stitch using two strands of embroidery thread. Each square represents one stitch over two fabric threads each way. When all the cross stitching is complete, add the outlining and the two rabbits' whiskers, nose and eyes in back stitch.

Press the completed work on the reverse using a hot iron setting (see p. 106). Fold the seam binding in half lengthwise and press in place. Position the seam binding around the edges of the lilac evenweave fabric, tack, then machine or back stitch it in place, folding it over on to itself diagonally at the corners for a neat finish.

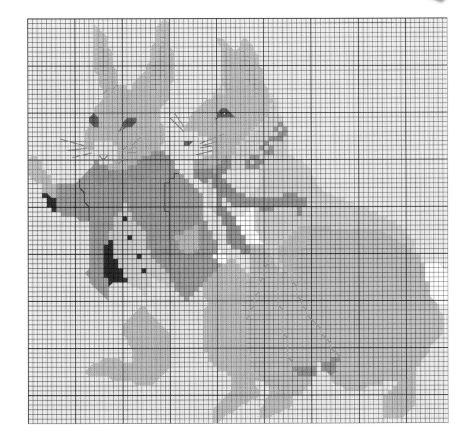

	DMC	Anchor		DMC	Anchor
▨	640	393	▨	502	877
▨	676	891	▨	3371	382
▨	931	921	▨	501	878
▨	932	343			
▨	316	969			
▨	3727	969		**Back stitch**	
▨	778	968		DMC	Anchor
▨	3033	830	▬	3371	382
☐	blanc	1	▬	501	878
			▬	316	969

Rabbit Cushion

A cushion will brighten up a nursery chair, particularly when adorned with this pretty rabbit motif worked mainly in soft blues and yellows.

Measurements

The actual cross stitch design measures 12 x 6cm
(4¾ x 2⅜in)
The cushion measures 40.5 x 40.5cm (16 x 16in)

Materials

• Two pieces of cream 28-count evenweave
fabric measuring 44.5 x 44.5cm (17½ x 17½in)
• DMC or Anchor stranded embroidery cotton,
one skein each of the colours shown in the chart
• Tapestry needle, size 26
• Cream sewing thread
• Sewing needle
• Length of piping cord measuring 5.5m (6yd)
used double
• Cushion pad measuring 40.5 x 40.5 cm or
41 x 41cm (16 or 18in)

To make up

Centre the design on one fabric piece (see p.104).

Following the chart and beginning centrally
(see p.104), work the design in cross stitch using
two strands of embroidery thread. Each square
represents one cross stitch over two threads of fabric each way. When all the cross stitching is
complete, work the eye and whiskers using dark
brown thread.

Press the completed work on the reverse using
a hot iron setting (see p.106), then make up the
cushion following the instructions on pp.106–7.

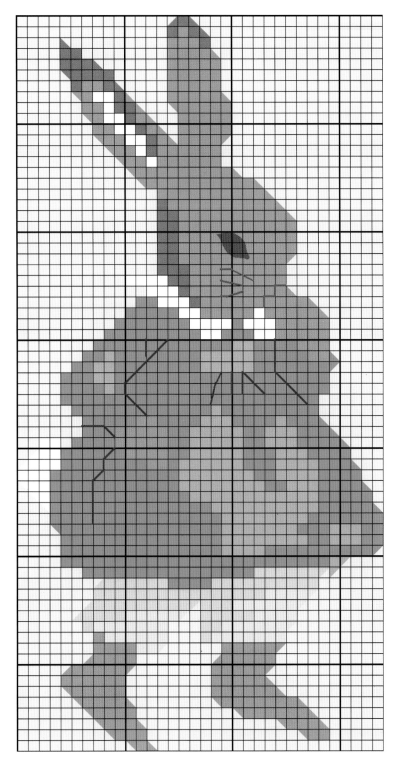

	DMC	Anchor		DMC	Anchor
	744	301	☐	blanc	1
	745	300	■	938	381
■	793	176		Back stitch	
	794	175		DMC	Anchor
	3032	903	▬	791	178
■	611	898	▬	938	381

TOYS & GIFTS